R is for Ruth

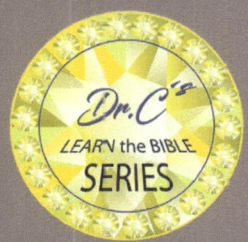

Dr. Cassundra White-Elliott

Illustrated by Palwasha Sajid

www.clfpublishing.org
909.315.3161

Cover design by Senir Design. Contact info: info@senirdesign.com

Illustrations by Palwasha Sajid of Fivver.com

ISBN #978-1-945102-76-9

Printed in the United States of America.

Dedicated to

All the students at Excellence Academy

A beautiful young woman named Ruth lived in a city called Moab. Ruth was married to Mahlon. He was the son of Naomi and Elimelech and the brother of Chilion. Sadly, Elimelech, the father died, and not too long after, Mahlon and Chilion died, too. Sadly, Ruth, her mother-in-law Naomi, and her sister-in-law Orpah were all left alone.

Ruth　　　　　**Orpah**　　　　　**Naomi**

Eventually, Naomi decided it was time for her to return back to her homeland, Bethlehem. She told each of her daughters-in-law to return to their own family. While one daughter-in-law decided to take Naomi's advice, Ruth decided it would be in her best interest to stay with Naomi. She told Naomi, "Your God will be my God, and your people will be my people."

So, Naomi and Ruth took the long journey to Bethlehem. When they arrived, they had to find a way to take care of themselves. They decided to look for a man named Boaz because he had a great field. He was Naomi's relative and was the kinsman redeemer. That is a person who helps out his family in their time of need.

Boaz

Boaz's field had many great crops, and he permitted Ruth to pick up morsels from the field that the harvesters left behind. After some time, Boaz asked the men about Ruth. He learned she was the daughter-in-law of Naomi. He also learned how she had shown her kindness to her mother-in-law. Boaz told the men to allow Ruth to gather as much as she wanted as she harvested with the other women.

Some time later, Naomi came up with a plan. She told Ruth to go to Boaz at night while he was asleep on the threshing floor. Ruth was to uncover his feet and lie down where his feet were. Ruth did exactly as she was told.
In the morning, when Boaz awoke, he saw Ruth and was surprised.

After that day, Boaz was very interested in marrying Ruth. But, there were rules a kinsman redeemer had to follow. There was another man who had the duty to redeem Ruth, so Boaz had to talk to him first to see if he was interested. After talking with the man, Boaz learned that the man was <u>not</u> interested. So, that gave Boaz the chance to marry Ruth.

After Ruth and Boaz were
married, they had a son. Naomi
was very happy because she
then had someone to love and
care for.

Boaz and Ruth's son was named Obed. Much later, he had a son named Jesse, who was the father of King David. From the line of King David came our Lord and Savior Jesus. Because of Ruth's willingness to go to a city she had never been because she loved her mother-in-law very much, she became part of a great family and from there, great people were born.